Best Practices

for Incorporating Building Science Guidance
into Community Risk MAP Implementation

November 2012

FEMA

Federal Emergency Management Agency
Department of Homeland Security
500 C Street, SW
Washington, DC 20472

This document was prepared by

URS Group, Inc.
12420 Milestone Center Drive, Suite 150
Germantown, MD 20876

Contract No.: HSFEHQ-10-D-0037
Task Order: HSFEHQ-11-J-0026

Table of Contents

Figures

Tables

Executive Summary

The Federal Emergency Management Agency's (FEMA's) mission is "to support our citizens and first responders to ensure that as a Nation, we work together to build, sustain, and improve our capability to prepare for, protect against, respond to, recover from, and mitigate all hazards."

In support of FEMA's mission, the Building Science Branch, which is part of the FEMA Federal Insurance and Mitigation Administration (FIMA) Risk Reduction Division, develops multi-hazard mitigation guidance that focuses on creating disaster-resilient communities to reduce the loss of life, number of injuries, and damage to property in natural and manmade hazard events. The Building Science Branch provides its technical services to FIMA, FEMA, other Federal agencies, States, and communities.

The Building Science Branch provides communities with guidance on reducing flood risk through publications, education, and tools that can be used with the Risk Mapping, Assessment, and Planning (Risk MAP) program to help communities implement hazard-resistant construction. The Risk MAP program is currently working with communities on Risk MAP projects, and at the completion of these projects, provides the communities with flood mapping products and flood risk assessment datasets that can be used to evaluate and enhance their mitigation plans. Building Science resources can be used in conjunction with Risk MAP products to strengthen the community's ability to reduce risk by increasing design standards for new construction and by implementing mitigation measures for existing construction. Members of the community can discuss the use of regulatory and non-regulatory Risk MAP products in conjunction with Building Science resources with Regional Building Science points-of-contact, other FIMA staff, and Risk MAP contractors during Risk MAP meetings.

The Risk MAP regulatory products are the Flood Insurance Rate Maps (FIRMs), Flood Insurance Studies (FISs), and FIRM databases. These regulatory products must be adopted by the community and incorporated into the community's floodplain management ordinance for it to participate in the National Flood Insurance Program (NFIP).

The key Building Science topics for regulatory and non-regulatory Risk MAP products are (1) increasing the community's risk awareness and (2) informing the community of the vast array of FEMA Building Science resources (publications, training, brochures, and websites). These products can benefit the community by increasing their understanding of floods and how to mitigate the risk. This information plays an important role in determining the appropriate standards for new construction, how existing structures can be retrofitted to reduce future flood damage, and the benefits of enhancing or updating building codes to reduce the community's risk.

Similarly, non-regulatory Risk MAP products can focus on specific aspects of building science data. The non-regulatory products are developed from the non-regulatory data sets developed during a project. Datasets from a project can be:

- A Changes Since Last Flood Insurance Rate Map dataset, which shows new floodplain areas or existing floodplain areas that may have a higher risk than previously indicated

- Depth grids and velocity grids, which provide details on locations and associated risk

- A Flood Risk Assessment dataset, which contains flood loss estimates to help the community focus on potential mitigation efforts

- An Areas of Mitigation Interest dataset, which has a series of GIS layers that show flood risk.

The datasets developed during a project are provided to the community, and the information allows the community to determine whether the higher risk areas require more stringent building codes.

Both regulatory and non-regulatory products are presented to the community in a series of Risk MAP meetings. The meetings also include information about Building Science Branch resources, such as the Building Science Toolkit CD, NFIP technical bulletins, disaster recovery advisories, building code assistance, web links, desk references, training resources, and technical publications, all of which can help the community meet FEMA's goal of fostering resilience through hazard-resistant structure design that leads to reducing the loss of life and property in hazard events.

ACRONYMS AND ABBREVIATIONS

AAL	Average Annualized Loss
AOMI	Areas of Mitigation Interest
ASCE	American Society of Civil Engineers
BFE	base flood elevation
CAZ	Coastal A Zone
CEO	community elected official
CCO	Consultation Coordination Officer
CRS	Community Rating System
CSLF	Changes Since Last FIRM
CTPs	Cooperating Technical Partners
FEMA	Federal Emergency Management Agency
FIMA	Federal Insurance and Mitigation Administration
FIRM	Flood Insurance Rate Map
FIS	Flood Insurance Study
FRA	Flood Risk Assessment
FRD	Flood Risk Database
FRM	Flood Risk Map
FRR	Flood Risk Report
GIS	Geographic Information Systems
H&H	hydrology and hydraulic
Hazus	Hazards U.S. (FEMA loss model)
HMA	Hazard Mitigation Assistance
I-Codes	International Building Codes
IBC	International Building Code
IRC	International Residential Code
LiMWA	Limit of Moderate Wave Action
LOMC	Letter of Map Change
NFIP	National Flood Insurance Program
PTS	Production Technical Services
RFC	Repetitive Flood Claims
Risk MAP	Risk Mapping, Assessment, and Planning
SFHA	Special Flood Hazard Area

SRL   Severe Repetitive Loss

GLOSSARY OF KEY TERMS

AOMI (Areas of Mitigation Interest) dataset. A non-regulatory Risk MAP dataset that provides data and information used to identify areas along flooding sources where potential flood mitigation projects may be beneficial.

Building Science Branch. Part of the FEMA Federal Insurance and Mitigation Administration Risk Reduction Division. Develops multi-hazard mitigation guidance.

BureauNet. A web-based database that contains information on all National Flood Insurance Program (NFIP) policies and claims since 1978.

Changes Since Last FIRM. See CSLF.

CSLF (Changes Since Last FIRM) dataset. Contains the changes in mapped floodplain and floodway boundaries and flood zone designations since the last FIRM and may include the addition of floodplain areas that were not previously identified.

CTP (Cooperating Technical Partner). Communities, regional agencies, State agencies, universities, and tribal nations participating in the Risk MAP program.

Discovery Map. Database of all spatial data collected up until the Discovery Meeting by the Risk MAP project team to present a project-wide picture of flood risk.

FIRM (Flood Insurance Rate Map). Shows floodplain and floodway boundaries; used in part to determine flood insurance requirements and premiums. Also referred to as an "NFIP map."

FIRM database. Digital flood-related data for a community, county, or watershed.

FIS report (Flood Insurance Study report). Regulatory report developed in conjunction with the FIRM. Contains the community's flooding history, engineering methods used to develop the FIRM, and flood profiles for studied flooding sources.

Flood Depth and Analysis Grids. Group of cells (i.e., raster dataset) that show flood risk in a variety of ways, such as depth, probability, or velocity of flooding in a particular location.

Flood Insurance Study report. See FIS report.

Flood hazard data. Regulatory data approved by FEMA that a community must adopt and incorporate into its floodplain ordinance in order to participate in the National Flood Insurance Program. Flood hazard data consist of the FIRM, FIS report, and FIRM database.

Flood risk. Likelihood that someone or something will be harmed when a flood hazard is encountered.

Flood Risk Assessment. See FRA.

Flood Risk Database. See FRD.

Flood Risk Datasets. Data that are used to produce the non-regulatory Risk MAP products (Flood Risk Database, Flood Risk Report, and Flood Risk Map). Flood Risk Datasets consist of Changes Since Last FIRM (CSLF), Flood Depth and Analysis Grids, Flood Risk Assessment (FRA), and Areas of Mitigation Interest (AOMI).

Flood Risk Map. See FRM.

Flood Risk Products. Non-regulatory Risk MAP products: Flood Risk Database, Flood Risk Report, and Flood Risk Map.

Flood Risk Report. See FRR.

FRA (Flood Risk Assessment). Non-regulatory Risk MAP dataset that provides flood loss data.

FRD (Flood Risk Database). Non-regulatory Risk MAP product that contains all the Flood Risk Datasets developed as part of the Risk MAP deliverables. The datasets include the technical support data for the FIS report and the GIS components of the FIRM.

FRM (Flood Risk Map). Non-regulatory, project-wide Risk MAP product that contains data from the FRD that depict flood risk including Hazus risk assessment results and selected AOMI. The FRM also includes the composite total 1-percent-annual-chance loss per census block as one of the GIS layers with losses per community.

FRR (Flood Risk Report). Non-regulatory Risk MAP product that is equivalent to the regulatory FIS report. The FRR summarizes information in the FRD and describes non-regulatory datasets and how they can be used for mitigation.

Preliminary FIRM. A draft FIRM presented to the community during the proposed NFIP Map Changes and Impact Meeting and used for the initial community review and public comment period.

Production Technical Services. See PTS.

PTS (Production Technical Services). FEMA contractor who obtains and coordinates data and develops comprehensive floodplain modeling, mapping, and GIS.

Risk MAP (Risk Mapping, Assessment, and Planning). FEMA program that provides selected communities with flood risk information, flood hazard assessment tools, and flood hazard mitigation planning support.

Risk MAP project. Risk MAP deliverables (regulatory and/or non-regulatory Risk MAP products). Not every Risk MAP project includes both regulatory and non-regulatory products.

Risk MAP project team. FEMA and Production Technical Services (FEMA mapping contractors).

SFHA (Special Flood Hazard Area). The land area covered by the floodwaters of the base flood on NFIP maps. The SFHA is the area where the NFIP's floodplain management regulations must be enforced and the area where the mandatory purchase of flood insurance applies.

Special Flood Hazard Area. See SFHA.

Study area. One or more watersheds included in a Risk MAP project.

SECTION ONE   INTRODUCTION

As the Federal Emergency Management Agency (FEMA) floodplain mapping program has evolved, Flood Insurance Study (FIS) data and maps have become more detailed and more accurate through improved computer models and greater use of Geographic Information Systems (GIS). In addition, the technical requirements of the FEMA Risk Mapping, Assessment, and Planning (Risk MAP) program have resulted in an expansion of the amount of useful flood data.

As the data have improved, the use of the data has extended beyond floodplain management permits and flood insurance. For example, the data are being used to increase the flood resistance in the design of new buildings and retrofits of existing buildings. Design information, which is available in the FEMA Building Science Branch library, includes enhanced design, siting, construction, and retrofit guidance and requirements for buildings in or adjacent to Special Flood Hazard Areas (SFHAs). The library consists of publications, technical bulletins, training descriptions, and tools, all of which are available online.

The flood risk data available from the Risk MAP program provides FEMA with additional resources to inform communities, property owners, and other interested parties about the vast library of Building Science resources. The resources can be used together with flood risk maps and other flood hazard products to reduce the loss of life, number of injuries, and property damage from flood events.

The purpose of this report is to present the best practices for incorporating Building Science flood mitigation information into the Risk MAP program and strategies for informing interested parties of the Building Science resources.

1.1   INTENDED AUDIENCE

The intended audience for this document consists of FEMA Headquarters staff, Regional Building Science staff, Regional Floodplain Management and Risk Analysis staff, Production Technical Services (PTS) contractors (FEMA mapping contractors), and Cooperating Technical Partners (CTPs). CTPs are communities, regional agencies, State agencies, universities, and tribal nations that participate in the Risk MAP program.

1.2   DOCUMENT ORGANIZATION

The document is organized as follows:

- Executive summary

- Acronyms and abbreviations

- Glossary of key terms – definitions of the key terms in this document; in the document, the first occurrence of terms defined in the glossary is in bold

- Section 1 – Purpose and need for the document, intended audience, and document organization

- Section 2 – Overview of the FEMA Building Science Branch

- Section 3 – Overview of the FEMA Risk MAP program, including its purpose and deliverables to the community (flood hazard information, flood risk assessment tools, and flood mitigation planning support)

- Section 4 – How to incorporate building science topics into regulatory Risk MAP products

- Section 5 – How to incorporate building science topics into non-regulatory Risk MAP

- Section 6 – How to incorporate building science topics into Risk MAP meeting preparation and the four primary Risk MAP meetings (Discovery, Flood Risk Review, Resilience, and Consultation Coordination Officer Meeting and Flood Map Open House)

- Section 7 – References and resources on hazard-resistant construction

SECTION TWO   FEMA BUILDING SCIENCE BRANCH

FEMA's mission is "to support our citizens and first responders to ensure that as a Nation, we work together to build, sustain, and improve our capability to prepare for, protect against, respond to, recover from, and mitigate all hazards."

The FEMA **Building Science Branch** is part of the FEMA Federal Insurance and Mitigation Administration Risk Reduction Division. In support of FEMA's mission, the Building Science Branch develops multi-hazard mitigation guidance that focuses on creating disaster-resilient communities to reduce the loss of life and property. The hazards the Building Science Branch deals with include natural and manmade. Natural hazards are naturally occurring events such as floods, earthquakes, hurricanes, high winds, and tornadoes that strike populated areas. Manmade hazards are events caused directly by deliberate or negligent human actions and include technological events (e.g., fire caused by faulty electronics) and acts of terrorism involving chemical, biological, radiological, or nuclear agents.

Damage from natural and manmade disasters can affect people both directly and indirectly. Direct effects are loss of life, injuries, and damage to homes, contents, and vehicles. Indirect effects are the temporary loss of businesses where goods and services are purchased, loss of the ability to get to and from work, loss of wages, and loss of public services.

The Building Science Branch supports the National Flood Insurance Program (NFIP),[1] Risk MAP program (see Section 3), and other national hazard mitigation programs. The support includes developing guidance, technical bulletins, disaster recovery advisories, building code assistance, technical publications, and training that will help communities meet FEMA's goals of fostering resilience through hazard-resistant structure design that leads to reducing the loss of life and property in hazard events.

The Building Science Branch helps advance mitigation practices in residences, businesses, and local communities through private-sector and stakeholder partnerships. The partnerships help educate corporate managers, employees, and customers. The target audiences of Building Science publications are design professionals for new and repaired structures, community permit and regulatory offices, small businesses, builders, homeowners, and renters.

For more information about the Building Science Branch, contact the Building Science Helpline at (866) 927-2104 or e-mail FEMA-Buildingsciencehelp@fema.dhs.gov. Allow up to 5 business days for a response.

---

[1] For information on the NFIP, see http://www.fema.gov/national-flood-insurance-program.

SECTION THREE   FEMA RISK MAP PROGRAM

The FEMA Risk Mapping, Assessment, and Planning (Risk MAP) program provides communities with (1) flood hazard information and flood risk assessment tools that can be used to update and enhance mitigation plans and (2) flood hazard mitigation planning and outreach support. Risk MAP strengthens the ability of communities to make informed decisions about reducing the flood risk through hazard mitigation and in new construction through higher design standards.

3.1   RISK MAP PROJECT AND PROJECT TEAM

A Risk MAP project provides a set of regulatory and non-regulatory Risk MAP products for a community. The project scope developed during the Discovery Phase determines which types of products will be developed. The Risk MAP project team consists of FEMA and the PTS.

3.2   RISK MAP DELIVERABLES

Risk MAP deliverables are the final flood data and mapping products provided to a community and consist of flood hazard information, mapping, and flood risk assessment tools. These are included in the Risk MAP regulatory and non-regulatory products (see Sections 3.2.1 and 3.2.2, respectively). The deliverables are provided to communities to enhance their understanding of the flood risks in their area.

3.2.1   Regulatory Risk MAP Products

Risk MAP regulatory products include the **flood hazard data** and consist of the Flood Insurance Rate Map (**FIRM**), FIS report, and FIRM database. Flood hazard data are regulatory because the community must adopt and incorporate the data into either their floodplain management ordinance in order to participate in the NFIP or their local building code in order to comply with the flood hazard provisions contained therein. Although the regulatory products contain limited data for building science, the community can use the floodway data table to obtain an average velocity for each cross-section. The community can also use the regulatory data to determine whether new and existing development is located in designated floodplains or regulatory floodways.

3.2.1.1   Flood Insurance Rate Maps

FIRMs are maps developed by FEMA to show flood hazards and risk. FIRMs show the designated 1-percent-annual-chance floodplain boundary (also known as the 100-year floodplain) and the regulatory floodways. Older FIRMs include base flood elevation (BFE) labels (in whole foot increments) and cross-section locations for referencing flood data to the FIS report. Newer FIRMs may show the BFE at each cross section in increments of 0.1 foot. The data can be overlaid on community or other base maps to facilitate use as a floodplain management map.

FIRMs are available online at the FEMA Map Service Center: https://msc.fema.gov

3.2.1.2 Flood Insurance Study Report

The **FIS report** accompanies the FIRM and provides flood information about the study area, which consists of one or more watersheds, and the technical methods that were used to develop the FIRM. Flood information includes bridge and dam locations, floodway widths, 1 percent-annual-chance flood elevations, velocity data, and plotted flood profiles of the flood elevations along the stream reaches that were studied.

Most FIS reports also contain the following:

- Flood discharge data at select points along each stream that was studied

- Profiles for the multi-frequency flood events that were studied

- In coastal FIS reports, a map of transect locations and data relating the coastal transects to the stillwater elevations and BFEs

- Floodway data including flooding source, cross-sections, and flood profiles; floodway width, area, and velocity; and regulatory elevations with and without the floodway

Upon release of the FIS report, property owners in new or existing floodplains should evaluate the flood elevations for their site to determine whether structures, or portions of structures such as foundations, exterior walls, and first floors, are susceptible to flooding or hydrostatic forces. For structures affected by floodwaters, mitigation measures that reinforce the foundation, protect the exterior, or prevent floodwaters above the first floor from entering the structure should be considered.

The FIS report can also benefit structures outside the 1-percent-annual-chance floodplain area by allowing a property owner to estimate the distance from the property to the floodplain boundary. For structures that are near the floodplain boundary and in an area with erodible soil, the property owner should consider whether the erosion potential is significant enough to result in floodwater, wave action, or hydrostatic forces that may affect the foundation or first floor of the structure.

3.2.1.3 FIRM Database

The **FIRM database** contains digital flood-related data that FEMA has developed for a community, county, or watershed. The database is used by the NFIP and enables FEMA, its contractors, and mapping partners to share data necessary for hydrology and hydraulic (H&H) modeling and FIRM production.

The FIRM database contains the technical support data for the FIRM and FIS. Communities can use the H&H modeling in the database to verify the potential hydrologic impacts of proposed development in the watershed or the potential hydraulic impacts of physical changes to the floodplain and floodway. The H&H modeling data combined with GIS overlay data and the FIRM base mapping allow the community to readily identify the areas and boundaries of any negative impacts from increases in flood elevations and floodplain areas that could result from proposed actions.

3.2.2 Non-Regulatory Risk MAP Flood Risk Products

The non-regulatory Risk MAP Flood Risk Products show or contain **flood risk** data and consist of the Flood Risk Database (**FRD**), Flood Risk Report (**FRR**), and Flood Risk Map (**FRM**). Communities are not required to adopt these products as part of their floodplain management ordinances but are advised to use them.

The Flood Risk Datasets used to develop the three non-regulatory Flood Risk Products are discussed in Section 3.2.2.1 and the Flood Risk Products are discussed in Section 3.2.2.2.

3.2.2.1   Flood Risk Datasets

Flood Risk Datasets represent a compilation of the data provided by the community and developed during the Risk MAP project and are used to produce the non-regulatory Flood Risk Products. Flood Risk Datasets can also be used in the following ways:

- To correct assumptions about flood depths and flow velocities in or near the floodway fringe if necessary. The assumptions are sometimes low. Even foundations outside the floodplain boundary and first floors above the base flood elevation (BFE) can be susceptible to wave action and flood depths greater than the 1-percent-annual-chance flood elevation.

- To allow permit officials, designers, structure owners, and contractors to make better, more informed decisions that will lower the flood risk for new or retrofit construction.

- To facilitate the enforcement of standards or enhanced building codes. Designing and constructing a project for the correct hazard is generally less costly than meeting the minimum code requirements and paying for repairs or large retrofit projects later on.

Flood Risk Datasets are divided into the following four categories: Changes Since Last FIRM (**CSLF**), Flood Depth and Analysis Grids, Flood Risk Assessments (**FRAs**), and Areas of Mitigation Interest (**AOMI**).

Changes Since Last FIRM Dataset

The CSLF dataset contains the increases and decreases in mapped floodplain and floodway boundaries and flood zone designations since the last FIRM (see **Figure 3-1**). The CSLF is produced only if the effective FIRM is digital or the mapped area is not shown on a previous FIRM.

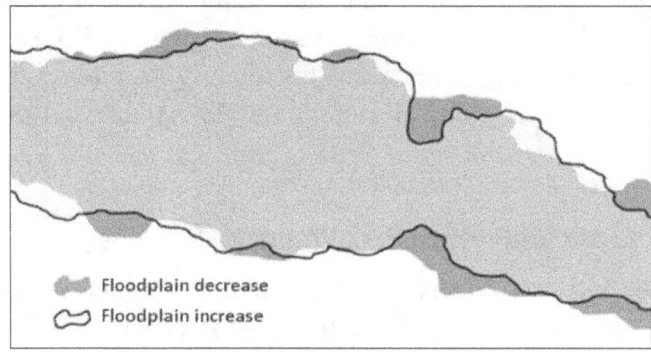

**Figure 3-1: Map showing changes since
the last FIRM (FEMA 2011c)**

Table 3-1 is a summary of the features, benefits, and intended users of the CSLF dataset.

**Table 3-1: Features, Benefits, and Intended Users
of the Changes Since Last FIRM Dataset**

Features and Benefits	Intended Users
• Identifies changes in floodplain and floodway boundaries and flood zone designations since the previous FIRM • Helps identify reasons for changes • Assists in prioritizing mitigation actions • Helps property and business owners determine their location relative to the mapped floodplain	• Community officials and leaders • Planners and developers • Engineers • Insurance agents, realtors, and lenders • Citizens

FIRM = Flood Insurance Rate Map

Flood Depth and Analysis Grids Datasets

The Flood Depth and Analysis Grids datasets show the depth and velocity of floodwaters and the probability that a particular location will be flooded over 1 year and over 30 years. A grid is a group of cells, and each cell shows the average value of the flood risk element in the area the cell represents.

Collectively, the Flood Depth and Analysis Grids datasets can be used to help identify and prioritize potential areas for mitigation based on risk, feasibility, and cost-effectiveness.

The Flood Depth and Analysis Grids datasets are as follows:

- **Flood Depth Grid** – depth of flooding at any given location in the floodplain (see **Figure 3-2**). For new Risk MAP projects, depth grids may include the 10-, 4-, 2-, 1-, and 0.2-percent-annual-chance flood events. Not all updated or new FISs have flood depth grids in the deliverables to the community.

- **Percent-Annual-Chance Probability Grid** – probability of flooding in any given year (true risk of flooding as a statistical probability). See **Figure 3-3**.

- **30-Year-Chance Probability Grid** – probability of a location being flooded during the life of a 30-year mortgage. Informing an owner with a 30-year

Figure 3-2: Simplified visualization of a Flood Depth Grid

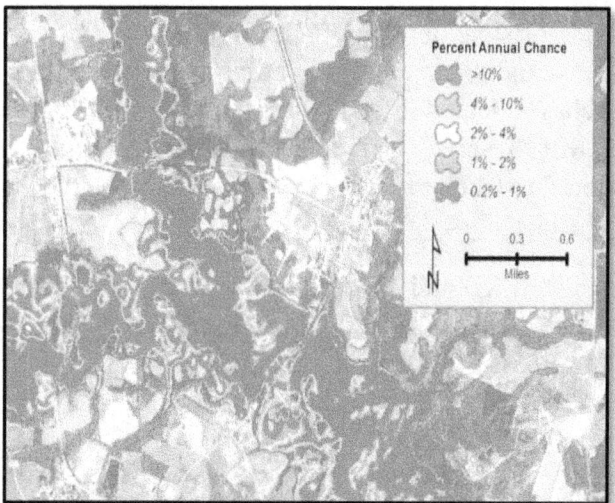

Figure 3-3: Percent-Annual-Chance Probability Grid showing flood risk (FEMA 2012a)

mortgage on a structure in the floodplain that the structure site has a 26 percent chance of flooding during the life of the mortgage is generally more effective than stating that the structure is in a 1-percent-annual-chance floodplain.

- **Water Surface Elevation Change Grid** – areas where the Risk MAP project resulted in changes to the calculated water surface elevations.

- **Velocity Grid** – floodwater velocity information that shows that hazards and risk vary across the floodplain. This information can be used to identify where building foundations in new or retrofit construction are at risk from higher velocity forces.

Table 3-2 identifies the features, benefits, and intended users of the Flood Depth and Analysis Grids datasets.

Table 3-2: Features, Benefits, and Intended Users of the Flood Depth and Analysis Grids Datasets

Features and Benefits	Intended Users
• Provides Flood Depth Grids for 10%-, 4%,- 2%,- 1%-, and 0.2%-annual-chance flood events • Provides percent annual chance of flooding in 30 years (common length of a mortgage); can be used to assist with mitigation prioritization based on risk	• Planners and developers • Local officials, including permit and construction inspection officials • Officials preparing mitigation grants • Home owners/home buyers • Construction professionals

Flood Risk Assessment Dataset

The FRA dataset relates flood risk to potential financial loss. This information can be used to increase flood risk awareness and to emphasize to property owners that they should take action to reduce the risk and purchase adequate flood insurance. The FRA dataset is based primarily on the Hazards U.S. (Hazus) MR4 Average Annualized Loss (AAL) Study and new refined Hazus analysis for new or updated flood study reaches. Information on Hazus is available at http://www.fema.gov/protecting-our-communities/hazus/.

The FRA data are stored in the FRD and are used to create the community-specific tables presented in the FRR, such as the example shown in **Figure 3-4**. **Table 3-3** identifies the features, benefits, and intended users of the FRA dataset.

	Total Inventory		Estimated Potential Losses for Flood Event Scenarios									
			10% (10-yr)		2% (50-yr)		1% (100-yr)		0.2% (500-yr)		Annualized ($/yr)	
	Estimated Value	% of Total	Dollar Losses	Loss Ratio	Dollar Losses	Loss Ratio	Dollar Losses	Loss Ratio	Dollar Losses	Loss Ratio	Dollar Losses	Loss Ratio
Residential Building and Contents Losses	$94,495,000	77%	$10,439,000	11%	$13,571,000	14%	$19,273,000	20%	$32,925,000	35%	$176,000	0%
Commercial Building and Contents Losses	$15,127,000	12%	$2,112,000	14%	$3,225,000	21%	$4,337,000	29%	$4,925,000	33%	$109,000	1%
Other Building and Contents Losses	$13,073,000	11%	$1,660,000	13%	$2,195,000	17%	$3,620,000	28%	$5,430,000	42%	$79,000	1%
Total Building and Contents Losses	$122,695,000	100%	$14,211,000	12%	$18,991,000	15%	$27,230,000	22%	$43,280,000	35%	$364,000	0%
Business Disruption	N/A	N/A	$760,000	N/A	$1,259,000	N/A	$2,011,000	N/A	$4,074,000	N/A	$18,000	N/A
TOTAL	$122,695,000	N/A	$14,971,000	N/A	$20,250,000	N/A	$29,241,000	N/A	$47,354,000	N/A	$382,000	N/A

Figure 3-4: Sample Hazus flood loss estimates (FEMA 2012b)

**Table 3-3: Features, Benefits, and Intended Users
of the Flood Risk Assessment Dataset**

Features and Benefits	Intended Users
• Identifies areas of higher flood risk by census block • User-defined facilities data (Hazus Level 2) can be used to refine building and contents losses when local data is available • Estimates potential future flood losses to existing structures • Improves ability to identify effective mitigation actions, mitigation plan updates, or areas requiring higher building code standards or flood-resilient designs and materials	• Planners and developers • Community officials • Emergency managers

Areas of Mitigation Interest Dataset

The AOMI dataset identifies areas that may benefit from flood mitigation. Similar to the engineering factors associated with the CSLF dataset, the AOMI dataset identifies physical factors that may contribute to flooding and losses. The primary sources of the AOMI dataset are:

- Data in local mitigation plans provided by the community and data provided by local stakeholders

- Engineering data from revised H&H models or other flood studies

- Federal Government data (e.g., residential and non-residential flood insurance claims)

Table 3-4 identifies the features, benefits, and intended users of the AOMI dataset.

**Table 3-4: Features, Benefits, and Intended Users
of the Areas of Mitigation Interest Dataset**

Features and Benefits	Intended Users
• Identifies areas at risk of flooding, along with the factors that contribute to those risks • Informs decision makers on where mitigation actions or additional building code requirements are needed or further research is warranted • Useful in formulating building code enhancements, prioritizing mitigation actions, and identifying needed resources	• Community officials • Planners and developers • Engineers • Citizens

3.2.2.2   Flood Risk Products

The four Flood Risk Datasets discussed in Section 3.2.2.1 are used to create three non-regulatory Flood Risk Products, which communities can use to help develop mitigation plans and comprehensive plans. The non-regulatory Flood Risk Products are the FRD, FRR, and FRM.

Flood Risk Database

The FRD includes the following:

- Tables and spatial data associated with the four Flood Risk Datasets

- Additional images and background spatial data used for the Flood Risk Map

- Additional images and tabular data for the Flood Risk Report

Table 3-5 identifies the features, benefits, and intended users of the FRD.

Table 3-5: Features, Benefits, and Intended Users of the Flood Risk Database

Features and Benefits	Intended Users
• Serves as the "container" for the four Flood Risk Datasets (CSLF, Flood Depth and Analysis Grids, FRA, and AOMI) • May be used to facilitate visualization of flood risk using the four Flood Risk Datasets	• GIS departments • Planners • State staff

AOMI = Areas of Mitigation Interest	FRA = Flood Risk Assessment
CSLF = Changes Since Last FIRM	GIS = Geographic Information System

Flood Risk Report

The FRR provides communities with a summary of the flood risk data that can be used for outreach and to improve risk and vulnerability assessments in mitigation plans. The FRR is the non-regulatory Risk MAP equivalent of the regulatory FIS report.

Table 3-6 identifies the features, benefits, and intended users of the FRR.

Table 3-6: Features, Benefits, and Intended Users of the Flood Risk Report

Features and Benefits	Intended Users
• Provides communities with a high-level summary of flood risk for either a single watershed or the project area that may be included in a mitigation plan • Provides detailed flood risk information on specific areas • Helps prioritize mitigation actions and resources	• Community officials and leaders • Planners • Engineers • Emergency managers

Flood Risk Map

The FRM (see **Figure 3-5**) contains data from the FRD that depict flood risk including Hazus risk assessment results and selected AOMI. The FRM provides communities with a high-level flood risk overview of the project area to enable them to identify flood risk hot spots and AOMI to facilitate coordination with neighboring upstream and downstream communities. The FRM also includes the composite total 1-percent-annual-chance loss per census block with losses per community as one of the GIS layers. Community officials may also create their own customized maps from within the FRD.

Table 3-7 identifies the features, benefits, and intended users of the FRM.

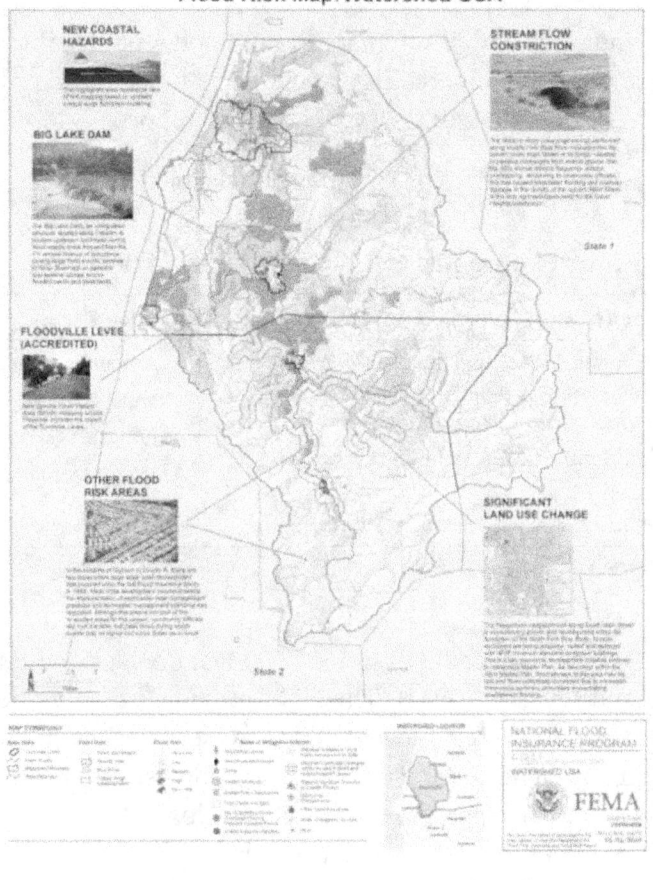

Figure 3-5: Example of a Flood Risk Map

Table 3-7: Features, Benefits, and Intended Users of the Flood Risk Map

Features and Benefits	Intended Users
• Depicts the flood risk in a watershed	• Community officials
• Provides areas of focus for community consideration	• Floodplain managers
• Shows the relationship of flooding issues across jurisdictions within a watershed	• Emergency managers
	• Developers
• Combines multiple datasets from the FRD into one map	• Planners
	• Citizens

FRD = Flood Risk Database

3.3   RISK MAP PHASES AND MEETINGS

3.3.1   Risk MAP Phases

A Risk MAP project has seven phases during which the PTS develops data and the Risk MAP project team presents the draft and final data to the community at the required Risk MAP meetings. Phase durations are determined by the Risk MAP project team. A project may require from 3 to 5 years for completion. The seven phases are:

A. **Planning and Budgeting:** Initial layout of the project, including identification of the watersheds and streams proposed for study and development of an initial budget. This is based on available resources and occurs prior to a formal meeting with the community.

B. **Discovery:** Initial coordination meeting that includes the presentation of the Discovery Map, draft project plan for the Risk MAP deliverables, and draft project charter. The primary objectives of the Discovery phase are to develop all possible local data, engage watershed stakeholders, understand community needs, and prepare a document that summarizes the decisions made at the Discovery Meeting.

C. **Data Development and Sharing:** Phase in which all analyses associated with developing the Flood Risk Products are developed. This phase includes an optional, but strongly recommended, Flood Risk Review Meeting that includes the presentation of the preliminary non-regulatory Risk MAP Flood Risk Products (FRD, FRR, and FRM).

D. **Risk Awareness and Mitigation Outreach:** Resilience Meeting to review potential actions for incorporation into mitigation plans.

E. **Proposed NFIP Map (FIRM) Changes and Impacts:** Changes since the last FIRM and impacts of the changes.

F. **Preliminary NFIP Map (FIRM) Release and Mitigation Planning.** Consultation Coordination Officer (CCO) meeting and Flood Map Open House.

G. **Due Process and Path Forward:** Presentation of the final regulatory and non-regulatory Risk MAP Flood Risk Products (FRD, FRR, and FRM) and issuance of the Preliminary FIRM.

Figure 3-6 presents the Risk MAP phases, meetings, and an example timeline. Project timelines vary based on the scope of the project, study area size, complexity, number of meetings, and the community's schedule.

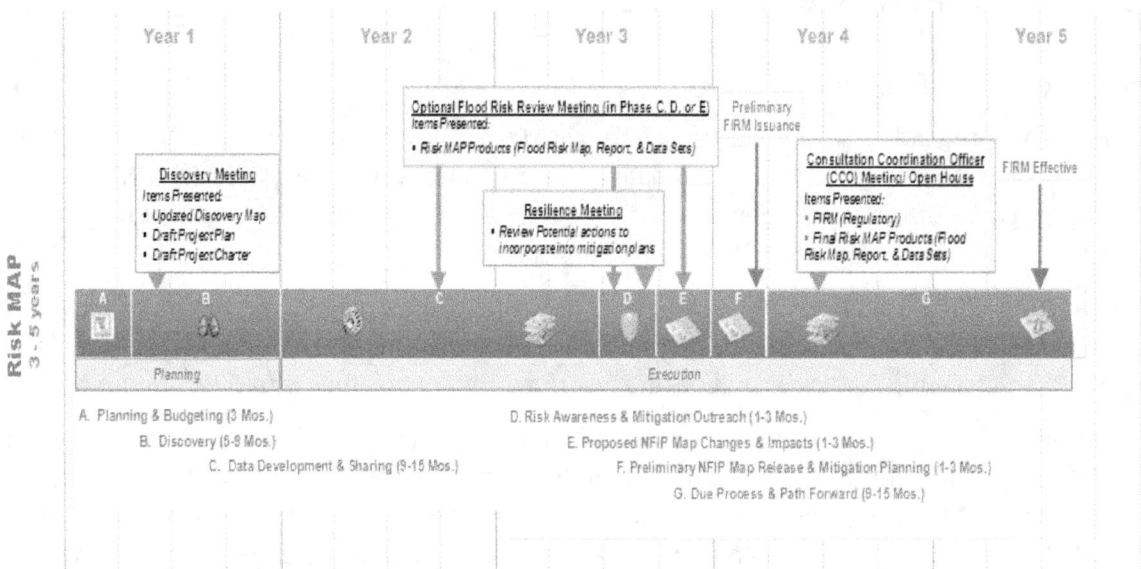

Figure 3-6: Risk MAP phases, meetings, and an example timeline

3.3.2 Risk MAP Meetings

The Risk MAP approach to community engagement includes creating partnerships with communities, documenting project objectives, and keeping communities apprised of the project status. Community engagement is fostered by meetings with the community and other stakeholders during the Risk MAP project, as described below.

3.3.2.1 Discovery Meeting

The Discovery Meeting is held after the existing flood modeling, mapping, and GIS data have been collected.

3.3.2.2 Flood Risk Review Meeting (Optional)

The Flood Risk Review Meeting is optional but *strongly* recommended if appropriate for the project. This is a technical/engineering meeting that gives community officials the opportunity to review the draft non-regulatory Risk MAP Flood Risk Products (if included in the project).

3.3.2.3 Resilience Meeting

The Resilience Meeting is one of several watershed-wide meetings that the project team has with community officials and other key stakeholders. This is the best meeting for Building Science staff and the communities to discuss not only mitigation options but also FEMA resources in the form of guidance, technical publications, training, and tools that can help the stakeholders address community-specific risks.

The objectives of the Resilience Meeting are to help communities understand flood risk, strategies they can use to reduce the risk and improve their community resilience to floods in the watershed, and the FEMA resources available to help them implement the strategies.

3.3.2.4   Consultation Coordination Officer Meeting and Flood Map Open House

The objectives of the CCO Meeting and Flood Map Open House are to formally present the preliminary maps to the community, reinforce use of the Risk MAP products, provide updates to mitigation plans (as discussed during the Resilience Meeting), and solicit commitments to act. The meeting and open house may be held together or separately.

SECTION FOUR   INCORPORATING BUILDING SCIENCE INTO REGULATORY RISK MAP FLOOD RISK PRODUCTS

The FIS report, the FIRM, and the FIRM database are provided to the community to help them meet their obligations under the NFIP. The most important reason for using an FIS report in conjunction with the FIRM is to determine whether a site is located in a 1-percent annual-chance floodplain, a Zone V, or a floodway, and to determine the BFE for that site.

The data in the FIS report are consistent with the accompanying profiles and FIRM. For example, the base flood water-surface elevation at each identified cross-section can be found in the floodway data tables in the FIS report, read from the flood profiles, and interpolated from the FIRM. Similarly, the distances between cross-sections, or their distance from identified reference points, can be found using any of the above data sources. The elevations of the computed profiles in the FIS report are used with ground elevation data to determine the limits of the flood zones shown on the FIRM. Again, flood elevations can be determined at any location along the studied stream using either the flood profiles or the FIRM.

Community officials can use the FIS data and structure location data to verify whether existing or proposed structures are within the boundaries of the 1-percent-annual-chance floodplain. The flood boundaries for a site are based on a comparison of the site BFE and other flood elevations and the site topographic data. The floodway boundaries for a site are scaled from the FIRM by measuring the width of the floodway from the watercourse centerline to the boundary edge on the FIRM and then using the same width, adjusted for changes in scale, on the site map.

The community can also see the positive effects from reduced flood elevations and floodplain areas from proposed mitigation measures. The purpose of flood mitigation is to reduce future flood damage. Some mitigation measures protect structures from flooding (e.g., by elevating the structure), and some lower flood elevations or alter the physical characteristics of the floodplain. Mitigation measures aimed at the more frequent floods (e.g., 25-year or 4-percent-annual-chance flood or less) are often feasible and cost effective even though they do not lower flood elevations.

SECTION FIVE   INCORPORATING BUILDING SCIENCE INTO NON-REGULATORY RISK MAP FLOOD RISK PRODUCTS

This section focuses on how to incorporate Building Science guidance into non-regulatory Risk MAP products (see Section 3.2.2 for a discussion of non-regulatory Risk MAP products). Building science focus topics are identified for the Flood Risk Datasets but not the Flood Risk Products. Non-regulatory Risk MAP products help to identify flood risks in ways that are different from the regulatory FIRM, FIS report, and FIRM database. Non-regulatory Risk MAP Flood Risk Products are more flexible and have more data than regulatory datasets. The additional data makes the non-regulatory datasets useful in the design of hazard-resistant construction. Resources and guidance on hazard-resistant construction are listed in Section 6 and available through the FEMA Library at http://www.fema.gov/search/site/FEMA%2520Library and searching on either "hazard-resistant construction" or "resilient construction."

Non-regulatory datasets such as depth and velocity grids provide data that can be used when addressing Building Science issues such as foundation design and community resilience. Other datasets such as the FRA dataset, which contains the Hazus analysis, can provide general information about geographic locations that have higher relative flood risk and the potential need for greater emphasis by local building officials.

Non-regulatory Risk MAP Flood Risk Products also highlight the areas where actions could reduce flood risks. For new construction, actions include correctly implementing the flood-related building codes and regulations by taking into account considerations such as high velocity or locations with past erosion or scour problems. Existing construction can also benefit from non-regulatory data that lead to mitigation actions. The AOMI dataset focuses on mitigation actions by providing a standard means of storing information about mitigation successes, locations with histories of flood loss, and locations that may be a concern in the future.

This section also addresses Building Science activities in areas affected by coastal flooding—Zone V (coastal areas subject to inundation by the 1-percent-annual-chance flood event with waves greater than 3 feet) and Coastal A Zones (CAZs) (wave heights between 1.5 and 3 feet). Areas with high-velocity waves have many unique building science considerations. Building Science publications such as FEMA P-55, *Coastal Construction Manual*, and FEMA 550, *Recommended Residential Construction in Coastal Areas*, contain relevant information.

In the following sections, one building science topic is discussed (focus topic in **bold type**) for each non-regulatory dataset and product. The focus topic is not the only building science topic that relates to the particular dataset or product; it is also a convenient way to bring building science concerns into the communication efforts related to the dataset or product. Focus topics provide a way to integrate building science concerns into presentations while reducing the potential for information overload for stakeholders. The sections also describe how each dataset and product can be used for risk identification and association mitigation actions.

5.1   FLOOD RISK DATASETS

5.1.1   Changes Since Last FIRM Dataset

The **Building Science focus topic for CSLF** involves the impacts of flood zone changes on new construction that may restrict use and increase code standards for an area.

The changes especially affect new construction in that current building practices may need to be changed because of the zone change. Although CSLF data are related primarily to identifying risk, the data can also be helpful in guiding potential permit or mitigation actions, especially when a Risk MAP study includes enhanced analysis such as integrating local structure location data. Structures that were in an unmapped area but are now in a zone such as a floodway or coastal Zone V are ideal candidates for mitigation and retrofit options.

5.1.1.1   Risk Identification

Some zone changes are have larger impacts than others and may include new maps of areas where no regulatory boundaries previously existed, new floodways in locations that previously had only unnumbered Zone A, and new coastal Zone V and Zone VE delineations with large horizontal (new land area) and/or vertical increase in BFE. Existing construction can also be affected when substantial damage occurs and structures have to be brought up to current codes. Although outreach may focus on new construction, the impacts on existing construction should also be considered.

Some Risk MAP projects may involve enhanced CSLF analysis using local structure data. The analysis would include primarily determining which existing structures have had zone changes. Tables may also be developed to summarize the total number of structures that have entered or left the SFHA for the community. For building science concerns, the more important results are the numbers and locations of structures with the more drastic zone changes. These structures could then be targets for individual or area mitigation activities.

In coastal areas, another consideration is the introduction on floodplain maps of the line for the Limit of Moderate Wave Action (LiMWA) and the associated designation of the Coastal A zone. The LiMWA line shows the inland limit of the area affected by waves taller than 1.5 feet. Research and post-disaster damage assessments have demonstrated that waves 1.5 feet or more high can induce significant structural damage.

Because the LiMWA line is currently considered advisory and not regulatory, the FIRM database does not include the LiMWA to establish SFHAs. Consequently, the LiMWA is not represented in the CSLF dataset. However, when localities adopt new floodplain ordinances to include new regulatory maps, they may also update their code provisions to have special building code requirements in the portion of the floodplain between the LiMWA and the boundary of the coastal Zone VE (greater than 3-foot waves). Therefore, when new mapping includes LiMWA lines, care should be taken to communicate the limitations of the CSLF dataset.

5.1.1.2 Actions

Drastic zone changes identified by the CSLF dataset may lead to several actions. The most prominent is the implementation of new building codes for new construction. Building code officials should be apprised of the requirements that will occur when the maps become effective. Structure foundation design, especially in areas with higher potential flow velocities, is greatly influenced by flood zone. This is especially true in coastal areas with wave action.

Mitigation and retrofits are other possible actions in areas with drastic zone changes. For low-lying areas with pre-FIRM construction, structure acquisition may be cost-effective. In areas with frequent flooding, structure elevation or elevation of utilities may be appropriate. Structures in coastal Zone V require elevation on piers, piles, or columns with open foundations to withstand wave actions. For riverine flooding with lower flood depth and flow velocities, dry and wet floodproofing may also be an option to reduce most flood-related damage.

5.1.2 Flood Depth and Analysis Grids Dataset

The **Building Science focus topic for the Flood Depth and Analysis Grids dataset** involves the impact that high depths and velocities have on foundation design and eligible floodplain construction.

The Flood Depth and Analysis Grids dataset provides grid or raster-based data describing the floodplain. Standard data requirements include flood depth grids for multiple return periods while enhanced data can include a water surface elevation and flood velocity grids. Although CSLF data provide a general indication of areas of concern with floodways and coastal Zone V, flood depth and velocity grids provide a more detailed view of where foundations need to be carefully designed.

5.1.2.1 Risk Identification

The Flood Depth and Analysis Grids dataset contains several grids that can aid building science efforts. One of these grids is the flood depth grid that provides estimates of flood depth for different return periods. Knowing not only where flooding may occur but also how deep the flooding will be can help form a more comprehensive picture of flood risks. Enhanced flood velocity data further sharpen flood risk issues and may show locations with a higher relative risk than the flood depth indicates.

As flood velocities increase, foundations need to be built to higher standards. Traditional enclosed foundations with footings and concrete masonry unit construction may need to be replaced with more disaster-resistant columns, piers, and piles with open foundations. One way these concerns can be communicated is by using local mitigation success stories in which these practices were implemented and performed well during flood events.

5.1.2.2 Actions

Because the Flood Depth and Analysis Grids dataset represents information as a detailed grid, focusing actions on specific locations is possible. When a community uses local structure location information as part of its Risk MAP project, the locations of interest can be specific to structures. For new construction, actions most often involve the building designs used to address more restrictive code requirements. If the depth and velocity grids show that a certain area within the SFHA has lower relative depths and velocities, development may be steered to this area rather than one with more restrictive design requirements.

5.1.3 Flood Risk Assessment Dataset

The **Building Science focus topic for the FRA dataset** involves the retrofit of structures and utilities.

The FRA dataset includes the results of analyses to determine how flooding affects the built environment. At a minimum, it includes the results of the AAL from a FEMA Hazus model analysis performed at the census block level. It may also include refined Hazus results that use new flood depth grids to improve loss estimates. Enhanced FRA datasets may include user-defined facilities analyses in which flood losses are calculated at the individual structure level.

Although the CSLF and Flood Depth and Analysis Grids datasets identify primarily high-risk areas, the FRA dataset assigns dollar values to the risks. The focus on retrofits, rather than on other types of mitigation, is intended to get homeowners and other structure owners thinking about what they can do to implement mitigation.

In some cases, retrofitting addresses most of the flood risk. In other cases, with complicating issues such as high velocities, retrofitting is not sufficient and other mitigation options such as acquisition are required. The "brick-by-brick" approach of introducing small pieces of information is less likely to intimidate average homeowners and may lead to more successful actions.

5.1.3.1 Risk Identification

The FRA dataset includes AAL data developed in 2010 as part of the Risk MAP program. Because the AAL data were developed using a Level 1 Hazus method, the data go down only to a census block level, which is screening-level flood risk information. However, the information that certain locations have a high likelihood of flood losses draws attention to these locations. The losses may be larger because the location has a high density of structures or larger depths or both.

In many Risk MAP projects, the AAL study can be supplemented by new refined Hazus analyses conducted within each Risk MAP study. The refined analysis uses flood depth information from a detailed engineering study that is run within Hazus. The new flood depth information used in the refined analysis provides a more accurate estimate of flood losses and further refinement of loss estimates. The refined analysis help steer attention to the locations where the majority of flood losses may be in existing structures.

Even when structure-specific data and losses are calculated, there should not be too much focus on absolute values. The most useful application of the FRA dataset is in the relative comparison of one part of the study area with another. The communication should be directed to mitigation actions and away from discussions on loss modeling limitations.

5.1.3.2 Actions

Retrofit actions are the focus topic for the FRA dataset. Retrofitting a structure using floodproofing practices is appropriate in some circumstances. Reviewing flood risk information from both the FRA and Flood Depth and Analysis Grids datasets can show whether floodproofing may work. Similarly, high flood losses from more frequent events, such as the 10-percent-annual-chance (10-year) flood event, may indicate that retrofitting using structure elevation would be cost-effective. Although not identical to a benefit-cost analysis, Hazus flood loss results provide a good indication of where mitigation may be appropriate. The FRA dataset includes annualized loss estimates, which take into account the multiple return period data to provide an AAL number for a location.

The FRA dataset focuses primarily on retrofit mitigation and can be expanded to all mitigation actions depending on the scope of the Risk MAP project. If an AOMI dataset is not included in a Risk MAP project, expanding the FRA dataset discussion to cover all building science-related mitigation actions would be appropriate.

5.1.4 Areas of Mitigation Interest Dataset

The **Building Science focus topic for the AOMI dataset** involves past and future mitigation as it relates to hazard-resistant construction and the reduction of damages. Communication should go beyond the retrofit focus of the FRA dataset and cover a broader set of mitigation actions.

The AOMI dataset is a collection of point features that provide supplemental information that can be helpful in hazard mitigation planning. The dataset also includes features that show where mitigation has been successful.

Table 5-1 contains a list of AOMI features and how they can be linked to building science topics related to mitigation.

Building Science publications that address known challenges to mitigation can also be a focus of communication. For example, FEMA 259, *Engineering Principles and Practices for Retrofitting Floodprone Residential Structures,* has detailed information on when floodproofing retrofit options can be successful and when they are not appropriate (e.g., when flood depths are more than 3 feet). This publication may provide answers to mitigation questions, and the questions may provide an opportunity to introduce the Building Science Publications Toolkit (see Section 5.1.1.2) and the FEMA Building Science website (http://www.fema.gov/building-science).

Table 5-1: Areas of Mitigation Interest Dataset Features

AOMI Feature	Building Science Mitigation Link
Dams	Downstream areas that may experience high velocities or increased flood depths
Levee and non-levee embankments	Residual risk areas on the landward side of levees that may experience high flood depths
Areas where stream flow is constricted	Possible retrofit needs if constriction produces high velocities
Coastal structures	Impact of coastal structures on coastal flooding and wave impacts
Key emergency routes overtopped during frequent flood events	Building utilities that may be inundated when routes are flooded
At-risk critical facilities	Retrofit and other mitigation options
Past flood insurance claims hot spots	Locations where mitigation may be possible
Individual Assistance and Public Assistance claims	Locations where mitigation may be possible
Areas of significant land use change (recent past and proposed)	Locations where new construction may continue to occur
Areas of significant coastal or riverine erosion	Locations to mitigation options should be focused
Areas with mitigation successes	Examples that may help communicate mitigation options
Other miscellaneous flood risk or mitigation-related areas	Local building science concern not represented by another AOMI features

AOMI = Area of Mitigation Interest

5.2 FLOOD RISK PRODUCTS

5.2.1 Flood Risk Database

The FRD contains the spatial databases and associated tables for the four datasets. It also contains data used to populate tables in the FRR and spatial layers used for the FRM. The primary archive function of the FRD can be used to store the building science topics that are included in the datasets.

FEMA provides the minimum FRD standards in a 2012 draft version of Appendix O, *Format and Standards for Non-Regulatory Flood Risk Products* (FEMA 2012a), which will be added to an updated version of *Guidelines and Specifications for Flood Hazard Mapping Partners* (FEMA 2003). As part of enhanced data development, a community may decide to add supplemental tables and spatial databases to the FRD. For building science, the supplemental data could be used to store information such as more detailed H&H analysis data and building-specific construction practices databases to community Mitigation Assessment Team investigation results. Because it is non-regulatory and allows for local enhancements, the FRD has the flexibility to archive more than the standard regulatory datasets and products.

5.2.2　Flood Risk Report

The FRR summarizes information in the FRD and describes non-regulatory datasets and how they can be used for mitigation actions. In many ways, the default tables and text in the FRR address many building science concerns. However, like the FRD, the FRR may benefit from enhanced features to bring forth local issues of concern. For example, the LiMWA issue could be added to the CSLF section of the FRR. The standard text and descriptions in the FRR can also be adjusted as needed for building science concerns.

5.2.3　Flood Risk Map

The FRM is a Risk MAP project-wide map showing a subset of the spatial data in the FRD. Because of scale issues, the map is often limited as an analysis product but does show the most important issues in a Risk MAP project. The FRM includes call-out boxes in which topics of concern can be highlighted. Building science concerns can be integrated into the call-out boxes.

SECTION SIX   INCORPORATING BUILDING SCIENCE INTO RISK MAP MEETINGS

The Risk MAP community meetings provide multiple opportunities for FEMA to help the community inform stakeholders about design and construction guidance and resources available from the FEMA Building Science Branch for moving toward disaster-resistant structures.

These meetings provide the Regional Building Science staff the best opportunity to reach the target audiences for their publications and inform communities how FEMA can help them address their hazards through tested approaches that were developed and reviewed by construction and design experts.

The four primary Risk MAP meetings are Discovery (required), Flood Risk Review (optional), Resilience (required), and CCO and Flood Map Open House (required).

Although all Risk MAP meetings provide opportunities to share technical guidance, the Discovery and Resilience Meetings provide the best opportunities. The Discovery Meeting is the project scoping meeting with community officials where they gain an understanding of the size and extent of their hazards. The Resilience Meeting is later, after new data have been shared with the community, and includes an audience from a wider area in the watershed. The Resilience Meeting is targeted to provide technical assistance for updating mitigation plans.

6.1   PRE-MEETING PREPARATION

6.1.1   Information Gathering

The information that should be gathered before the Discovery Meeting consists of flooding-related information about the community and a list of relevant Building Science resources.

6.1.1.1   Pre-Meeting Community Reconnaissance

Before any of the Risk MAP meetings, the participating Building Science staff should gather background information on the community that includes flooding history, current needs based on size (area and population), flooding problems, historical damage, level of interest in addressing flood problems, mitigation activities, and FEMA or State mitigation grants. Building Science staff should coordinate with the Risk MAP project team regarding community information and flood data that have already been assembled.

Although all of the needed data may not be readily available prior to the Discovery Meeting, the data that can be obtained and reviewed before the meeting will prepare Building Science staff for the community flood issues. The reconnaissance discussed here is not intended to replace or reduce the need for the Discovery Meeting but rather to provide FEMA attendees with an educated and solid background on the community and its flooding issues prior to the first formal community meeting.

Table 6-1 contains the types of information that may be helpful to have during Risk MAP meetings.

Table 6-1: Pre-Meeting Community Reconnaissance

Information	Purpose of Gathering the Information
Flood studies – effective FIS and maps, LOMC history, best available data approvals by FEMA, flood studies by Federal or State agencies	Provides size and extent of the community flooding problems, types of flooding (riverine, coastal, alluvial fan), and previous and new development areas
Community statistics – population, community area (square miles), number of watersheds, number of river or stream miles within corporate limits, location of critical facilities, growth areas based on 1-year and 5-year permit activity	Assesses adequacy of effective FIS, estimated lengths of new or restudied areas and sufficiency of study funds, additional information on current flood problems, and areas of recent development
Community hazard mitigation plan	Demonstrates the community's understanding of its flooding problems, historically floodprone areas, and proposed mitigation measures
Number of flood insurance policies in effect and number of past flood claims	Verifies scope and extent of the community flooding problems; a history of flood insurance claims may indicate a lack of resources to address the flooding problems
Number of RFC and SRL properties in the community	Provides data on the amount and extent of historical flooding damage
Local officials' knowledge of where flooding problems exist	Identifies limitations or omissions of floodplain areas on current FIRMs, and potential areas for future mitigation activities especially if flood elevations increase
Previous mitigation projects – type, number, areas where mitigation was implemented, and success stories	Verifies community interest in addressing its flood problems and a willingness to commit its funds; the type of mitigation measures implemented may indicate a preference for mitigation types
CRS rating	The CRS rating provides the minimal type and extent of CRS activities, indicates the community level of interest, and identifies stormwater reduction measures
Current building code including the name and date the model code that was adopted, additional requirements, and date of last update	Identifies and provides detailed information on the minimum requirements for all new construction and retrofits and indicates likely provisions for code enhancement for use of flood-resistant materials and designs
Building Science resource needs assessment – hazard type, building code status, and number of flood claims and other available data	Identifies the Building Science publications and websites that would be useful for the community

CRS = Community Rating System
FEMA = Federal Emergency Management Agency
FIS = Flood Insurance Study
FIRM = Flood Insurance Rate Map

LOMC = Letter of Map Change
RFC = Repetitive Flood Claims
SRL = Severe Repetitive Loss

The recommended resources to take to the meetings are as follows:

- Effective FIS, FIRMs, and LOMC history

- Community statistics on the quantity and location of critical facilities

- Number of flood policies in effect and total claims paid by disaster (access to the FEMA BureauNet or the Community Information System may be necessary)

- Number of Repetitive Flood Claims (RFC) and Severe Repetitive Loss (SRL) properties (access to the FEMA BureauNet or the Community Information System may be necessary)

- Current building code in effect

- Building Science needs assessment

6.1.1.2 FEMA Building Science Resources

The Building Science website, http://www.fema.gov/building-science and the Building Science Toolkit CD provide stakeholders with access to a large number of free publications, technical guidance documents, design requirements, and hazard-resistant material and building code information that are related to flooding and other natural hazard design, construction, and mitigation. The Toolkit contains more than 50 publications and contains information that can be used by elected officials, local permit officials, residents, businesses, renters, structure owners, design professionals, and contractors.

The Toolkit is organized by hazard and contains a list of publications relevant to natural hazards. In addition to the table of contents, the Toolkit has a multi-tabbed spreadsheet titled "FEMA Building Science Publications for Risk MAP Outreach" that lists titles, descriptions, and links to additional Building Science publications that are available online.

Included on the Toolkit are FEMA summaries of the flood-resistant provisions of the 2009 and 2012 International Building Codes (I-Codes) and additional building code resources and web links.

Recommended meeting handouts include the following:

- Copies of the Building Science Toolkit CD

- Hard copies of the Toolkit table of contents (to present materials on the CD)

- Hard copies of the Toolkit spreadsheet tab(s) applicable to the community's natural hazard(s) (to focus on resources relevant for the community based on hazard)

6.1.2　Project Communication

6.1.2.1　Understanding the Needs of Local Officials and Stakeholders

FEMA staff should recognize that the local officials and stakeholders who attend the Discovery, Resilience, and other meetings may know considerably less about flooding, flood mapping, and regulatory requirements than the Risk MAP project team. Therefore, the FEMA staff that attend the meetings should be prepared to discuss flooding and mapping in basic terms. The stakeholders will most likely have more credibility for and pay more attention to the local officials than to FEMA staff. Any relationships that were developed and discussions that occurred before the pre-Discovery Meeting may be beneficial when FEMA staff try to convince stakeholders who have not been flooded or have never seen a flood in their community that they may still be at risk from flooding and associated hazards such as high velocities and potential scour or erosion.

Floodplain mapping provides the tools necessary to identify not only areas where mitigation would be useful but also areas where future construction should either be prohibited or regulated through enhanced building codes and permit requirements.

6.1.2.2　Flood Hazard Mitigation

Mitigation is defined as a sustained action that reduces the long-term risk and severity of a hazard's effects on people and property. Flood mitigation is a means of managing the risk and damage from flooding. This mitigation is essentially a community effort, based on the frequency of the hazard and the risk posed for the built environment.

The two basic types of flood mitigation are:

- **Structural flood mitigation** – involves the design and construction of structures and other physical or manmade improvements that alter the natural floodplain or flow characteristics to control the flow and amount of water. Examples are dams, levees, floodwalls, detention and retention facilities, structure elevations, and drainage improvements. Structural mitigation tends to be more expensive than nonstructural mitigation and may require maintenance and human intervention to operate. It may also provide a false sense of protection while also promoting floodplain development.

- **Nonstructural flood mitigation** – involves administrative actions (acquisition) and tools (ordinances and building codes) that do not depend on controlling the flow of water. Nonstructural methods emphasize controlling activities that could result in increased flood damage. Examples are floodplain management ordinances, enhanced building codes, land-use planning, and best practices for land development. Generally, nonstructural methods are less expensive and can provide more long-term reduction in flood damage than structural mitigation measures.

Local officials and other stakeholders may not fully understand the need for mitigation or that mitigation comes in different sizes, costs, and levels of effectiveness. They may believe that mitigation is reserved for large flood control projects and that they should not consider the more repetitive and less damaging flooding from lower frequency events between the 20-percent (5-year) and 4-percent-annual-chance (25-year) events.

The following are some of the common misconceptions about flood mitigation that FEMA staff should be prepared to address.

1. Only large flood control projects, such as dams and levees, are effective at mitigating flood damage.

2. Mitigation is unnecessary as long as residents can purchase flood insurance.

3. There has been no significant flood damage in our community in more than 10 (20, 25, 40, or 50) years.

4. FEMA will cover all costs after a disaster.

5. Only projects eligible for FEMA Hazard Mitigation Assistance (HMA) grants are effective.

6. Flood damage in our community is only from lower frequency flood events, and FEMA does not fund projects that address this type of damage.

7. Flood hazards are not addressed in building codes.

8. FEMA's HMA grant program requirements are too difficult to meet, the guidance is confusing, and the required FEMA Benefit-Cost Analysis is too difficult to prepare and complete.

FEMA attendees should also explain that mitigation based on hazard and risk may have some benefits even if the measure does not prevent all damage. Mitigation can range from individual lot and structural measures to large-scale projects that protect many residents and structures. Stakeholders also need to understand that mitigation measures that have low State or Federal priorities or that do not meet HMA programmatic requirements may still be feasible and effective if funded at the local level.

Table 6-2 is a list of potential mitigation options that the community may want to consider.

It is also important that local officials understand that flooding not only affects the built environment (structures, contents, and infrastructure) but also local services and utilities, the economy, people's routines, and their expectations of what the community should and will do for them after a disaster. The effects of flooding range from small inconveniences such as lawn and nuisance flooding and temporary road closures to large disasters that can result in injuries and fatalities, affect structure and contents, and affect community functions and services such as schools, hospitals, and police, fire, and emergency services.

It may be useful to share available information on mitigation projects in neighboring communities, elsewhere in the state, or in other communities of similar size and risk. Mitigation success stories can demonstrate the benefits of mitigation on different scales as well as provide a community-level point-of-contact for local officials.

The recommended meeting handouts are hard copies of the mitigation measures listed in Table 6-2.

Table 6-2: Potential Structural and Nonstructural Flood Mitigation Measures

Structural Flood Mitigation Measures	Nonstructural Flood Mitigation Measures
• Structure elevation	• Acquisition and structure demolition or relocation
• Full or partial dry floodproofing of structures	• Protecting/elevating service equipment
• Full or partial wet floodproofing of structures	• Flood warning system for individual property
• Stormwater detention or retention facilities	• Automated flood notifications (phone calls, e-mails, social media)
• Stormwater system control	• Public education
• Levee/floodwall protection for multiple structures	• Flood insurance
• Dams	• Floodplain management ordinance that exceeds the minimum requirements of the NFIP
• Drainage improvement projects	• Land-use planning
• Levee/floodwall for a single structure	• Zoning and subdivision ordinances
	• Enhanced or updated building codes that exceed the minimum State requirements
	• Stormwater best practices for land development

6.1.2.3 Project Website

Because a Risk MAP process can take 3 to 5 years to complete and because of the potential for personnel turnover during that time, a community website can be useful for local officials, residents, and FEMA as a central repository for project-related data and information. A project website should be created and accessible by all project stakeholders. Before launching a project website, FEMA and the community need to decide on the content and who will have privileges for uploading and revising website content.

The contents of the project website may include any of the following:

1. Project name, scope, purpose, and funding sources (but not funding amounts)

2. Project status and a calendar of upcoming key steps or meetings

3. Community Risk MAP project contacts (names, e-mail addresses, and phone numbers)

4. Background on community flooding issues, number of flood insurance policies in effect, and the financial value of past flood insurance claims

5. Effective FIS report and FIRMs

6. Floodplain management ordinance and construction permit requirements

7. Community building code and planned changes

8. Community hazard mitigation plan

9. FEMA Risk MAP and Building Science Outreach materials

10. An area for stakeholder comments and stakeholder surveys regarding meeting formats, website content, and mitigation project priorities

11. Existing mitigation projects and mitigation success stories

12. Potential mitigation project types that are applicable for the community

13. Web links to applicable State, county, and community websites

14. Web links to useful FEMA websites including flood insurance, disaster recovery webpages, Building Science, FEMA building code resources, and information on downloading or ordering FEMA design manuals and additional copies of the Building Science Toolkit CD

6.1.2.4 Social Media

The community may also want to consider use of one or more social media outlets to advertise upcoming meetings (date, time, and location), provide project progress reports, and announce the names and source location of newly released project related materials. The advantages of using social media are that it is a low-cost, easy, and fast way to keep residents and the Risk MAP Project Team informed. The primary concern with social media is that the responsibility for releasing new information must reside with a limited number of community staff to ensure that the information that is distributed is correct, accurate, and timely.

6.2 DISCOVERY MEETING

The Risk MAP requirements for the Discovery Meeting are provided in Appendix I, *Discovery* (FEMA 2011a), which will be added to an updated version of FEMA's *Guidelines and Standards for Flood Risk Analysis and Mapping* (FEMA 2003). The suggestions in this document for preparing for the Discovery Meeting are not intended to revise or circumvent the requirements in Appendix I. The intent is to provide suggested activities, materials, and useful data for consideration to prepare for participation in the meeting and include questions for the community, guidance, and handouts that can be used to show and discuss the Building Science resources available to the community.

The Discovery Meeting is the first required project meeting that the Project Team has with community officials and other key stakeholders. It is held at the beginning of the Discovery phase of the Risk MAP process and occurs after the study planning and budgeting process.

Coordination among the watershed stakeholders, including the community, FEMA, the State, and the PTS takes place prior to this meeting.

The community should formally request non-regulatory Risk MAP Flood Risk Products during the Discovery Meeting and should be prepared to discuss why the non-regulatory products are important and how the community plans to use the data. The non-regulatory datasets are (see Section 3.2.2.1):

- Changes Since Last FIRM
- Flood Depth and Analysis Grids
  - Flood Depth Grid
  - Percent-Annual-Chance Probability Grid
  - 30-Year-Chance Probability Grid
  - Water Surface Elevation Change Grid
  - Velocity Grid
- Flood Risk Assessment
- Areas of Mitigation Interest

Although the attendees at the Discovery Meeting may be more focused on the project start than what the final data may show, it is never too early to start considering mitigation activities or to start formulating ideas for updating the community mitigation plan. The FEMA or PTS project lead should hand out the Building Science Toolkit and provide a brief discussion (15 minutes) about the Toolkit and the benefits of starting the mitigation evaluation process at this time.

Table 6-3 provides information on the various elements of the Discovery Meeting.

Table 6-3: Elements of the Discovery Meeting

Element	Description
When held	First of four community Risk MAP meetings. Occurs during the Discovery Phase.
Objectives	• Introduce watershed stakeholders to each other • Discuss sources of new and existing data • Review initial mitigation opportunities and priority study areas • FEMA determines whether the community wants and needs the non-regulatory datasets • Community formally requests non-regulatory Risk MAP products such as depth and velocity grid data
Recommended meeting attendees	• FEMA and the PTS • State National Flood Insurance Coordinator • State Hazard Mitigation Officer • Community CEOs or tribal leaders and floodplain managers • Local planner and economic development contacts

Element	Description
Meeting activities	• FEMA leads an interactive discussion where communities state what is important to them
	• Meeting participants must own recommendations resulting from the meeting
	• Share and review the Discovery Map (database of all spatial data collected so far) with communities to show a watershed-wide picture of flood risk
Building Science objectives	The FEMA or study lead should handout the Building Science Toolkit CD and provide a brief discussion (15 minutes) on the benefits of considering mitigation needs and opportunities at this time.

CEO = community elected official PTS = Production Technical Services
FEMA = Federal Emergency Management Agency Risk MAP = Risk Mapping, Assessment, and Planning

Providing Guidance to Local Officials and Stakeholders

The Discovery Meeting should be treated as a listening session for the FEMA attendees. The FEMA staff can target ways to help the community understand the Risk MAP objectives and how Building Science resources can help them with future construction, siting, and building code requirements. The discussion and interaction should help broaden the community interest while getting the attendees more engaged and moving the mitigation discussion along at this and future meetings.

6.3 FLOOD RISK REVIEW MEETING

The Flood Risk Review Meeting is an optional but strongly recommended meeting. This is the second of the community meetings and has a technical focus that provides the community with the opportunity to review the draft Risk MAP products if they are included as part of the Risk MAP project scope. This meeting may also be important for Risk MAP projects that include significant changes in the identified hazard. The Flood Risk Review Meeting allows the project team to highlight the flood risk associated with the changes and gives communities the opportunity to review the results.

To encourage a discussion about flood risk, the Project Team should not present the regulatory Risk MAP products (FIRM, FIS, and FIRM database) or the non-regulatory Risk MAP datasets related to the CSLF at this meeting.

Table 6-4 provides a description of the elements of the Flood Risk Review Meeting.

Table 6-4: Elements of the Flood Risk Review Meeting

Element	Description
When held	Second of four community Risk MAP meetings. Occurs at the end of the Data Development and Sharing Phase.
Objectives	• Increase stakeholder understanding about the FRM, FRR, and FRD • Present community officials or tribal leaders with additional outreach opportunities to assist them in communicating Risk MAP products to citizens in affected communities • Gather information on the focus for the upcoming Resilience Meeting • Present draft Risk MAP products to the communities' technical stakeholders
Recommended meeting attendees	• FEMA and the PTS • State NFIP Coordinator and State Hazard Mitigation Officer • Other Federal or State agencies (as appropriate) • CEOs, tribal leaders, floodplain manager, engineer, building inspector, emergency manager • Mitigation planning team • Other key stakeholders (academic, regional planning, private-sector representatives)
Meeting activities	• Present the draft non-regulatory Risk MAP products • Discuss outreach tools and potential areas of the communities in need of flood risk outreach and communications
Building Science objectives	Although the Building Science objectives are better met at the Discovery and Resilience Meetings, the FEMA or study lead should be able to offer guidance and refer to the Building Science website or the Toolkit if the stakeholders want to discuss flood mitigation or find out additional information.

CEO = community elected official	FRR = Flood Risk Report
FEMA = Federal Emergency Management Agency	PTS = Production Technical Services
FRD = Flood Risk Database	Risk MAP = Risk Mapping, Assessment, and Planning
FRM = Flood Risk Map	

6.4 RESILIENCE MEETING

The Resilience Meeting is part of the Risk Awareness and Mitigation Outreach phase and is one of several watershed-wide meetings (and the second meeting required) that the project team has with community officials and other key stakeholders during a Risk MAP project. The intent is to build local capacity for implementing priority mitigation activities in the watershed. This can be accomplished by discussing the project status through a review of what has occurred since the Discovery Meeting to help the community better understand flood risk, ways to reduce the risk, the resources available to the community, and the importance of disseminating information about the flood risk to all the stakeholders.

This meeting should provide a comprehensive view of mitigation planning and mitigation options available to communities while also sharing potential mitigation actions that communities can initiate. This approach will result in a better understanding of how to leverage community activities, assets, and concerns in support of mitigation actions and to remove barriers or create incentives for mitigation action. Stakeholders can also review the previous list of AOMI to see how the new data affect these areas.

Table 6-5 provides information on the various elements of the Resilience Meeting.

Table 6-5: Elements of the Resilience Meeting

Element	Description
When held	Third of four community Risk MAP meetings. Occurs during the Risk Awareness and Mitigation Outreach Phase.
Objectives	The Project Team leads a review of the study and promotes an interactive discussion to: • Build local capacity for understanding and implementing mitigation activities • Review the flood risk • Discuss strategies to reduce the flood risk • Identify and review the resources available from FEMA and the State to help implement the mitigation strategies • The importance and opportunities for communicating flood risk to the constituents
Recommended attendees	• FEMA and the PTS • State National Flood Insurance Program Coordinator and State Hazard Mitigation Officer • Other Federal or State agencies that were involved or interested in the study results • Community and tribal officials including the CEO, floodplain manager, engineer, building inspector, mitigation plan team, emergency manager, and land-use decision makers • Other interested watershed stakeholders such as public infrastructure owners, property owners (high risk and otherwise), engineers and surveyors, and nongovernmental agencies • All individuals contacted during the Discovery process or who attended the Discovery Meeting
Activities	• Share and review the regulatory products and non-regulatory flood risk analyses and assessments to understand flood risk • Review the development types (residential, public, business, and infrastructure) in the increased floodplain areas • Review previous damage locations based on new data to determine the size of floodplain increases • Identify areas of high flood depth and velocities • Review strategies to reduce flood risk based on the AOMI, identify potential mitigation areas based on flood height and floodplain area increases, and share best practices • Highlight previous mitigation activities and mitigation success stories • Review mitigation and structure retrofit resources and distribute handouts that provide guidance on the selection, evaluation, and implementation of mitigation projects, including information on best practices • Discuss revisions needed to the local building codes and the community mitigation plans based on the new data

Element	Description
Building Science objectives	Because there may be attendees who are new to the Risk MAP process and an increase of mitigation interest is likely, FEMA or the study lead should hand out the Building Science Toolkit CD and provide a brief discussion (15 minutes) on the potential for mitigation to reduce damage.

AOMI = Areas of Mitigation Interest	FEMA = Federal Emergency Management Agency
CEO = community elected official	Risk MAP = Risk Mapping, Assessment, and Planning

Use of Building Codes to Promote Resilience

Communities that participate in the NFIP adopt regulations and codes that govern development in SFHAs and enforce the requirements through the issuance of permits. The International Residential Code (IRC) and International Building Code (IBC), by reference to the American Society of Civil Engineers (ASCE) 24, include requirements that govern the design and construction of buildings and structures in flood hazard areas. FEMA has determined that the flood provisions of the I-Codes are consistent with the requirements of the NFIP (the I-Code requirements meet or exceed NFIP requirements). ASCE 24, a design standard developed by the American Society of Civil Engineers, expands on the minimum NFIP requirements with more specificity, additional requirements, and some limitations.

The Building Science Branch regularly partners and coordinates closely with developers, building professionals, scientific organizations, the International Code Council, ASCE, and building or code standards committees to participate in, and often lead, the development and implementation of multi-hazard resistant building codes and standards. These partnerships have led to the successful incorporation of best practices and sound disaster-resilient policies into national model building codes and engineering standards that form the basis of the building regulations available for adoption and implementation by communities to reduce risks. FEMA building code resources are available at http://www.fema.gov/building-science/building-code-resources.

The following documents provide information concerning the flood-resistant provisions of the codes and are in the Toolkit (References 1-4) and available on the Building Science website (References 1-5).

1. *Flood Resistant Provisions of the 2012 International Code Series* (FEMA 2012c) – compilation of flood-resistant provisions, prepared by FEMA, of the 2012 International Code Series. Also included as a separate document is a summary of changes from the 2009 IBC. The 2012 edition of the I-Codes contains provisions that are consistent with the minimum flood-resistant design and construction requirements of the NFIP for buildings and structures.

2. *Flood Resistant Provisions of the 2009 International Code Series* (FEMA 2011b) – compilation of flood-resistant provisions, prepared by FEMA, of the 2009 International Code Series. Also included, as a separate document, is a summary of changes from the

2006 IBC. The 2009 edition of the I-Codes contains provisions that are consistent with the minimum flood-resistant design and construction requirements of the NFIP for buildings and structures.

3. *Highlights of ASCE 24-05 Flood Resistant Design and Construction* (FEMA 2010). ASCE 24-05 is a referenced standard in the IBC and IRC. Any building or structure that falls within the scope of the IBC that is proposed in a flood hazard area is to be designed in accordance with ASCE 24-05. The IRC requires that dwellings in floodways be designed in accordance with ASCE 24-05. The 2009 and 2012 editions of the IRC include an alternative that allows communities to require homes in Zone V to be designed in accordance with ASCE 24-05. Highlights of ASCE 24-05 that complement the NFIP minimum requirements are building performance, flood-damage resistant materials, utilities and service equipment, and siting considerations.

4. *Provisions of the 2009 I-Codes and ASCE 24 Compared to the NFIP* (FEMA 2011d) – comparison of the provisions of the 2009 I-Codes/ASCE 24-05 and NFIP requirements.

5. *CodeMaster for Flood Resistant Design* (S.K. Ghosh Associate 2011) – provides designers with an easy-to-use desk reference that identifies the flood provisions in the 2009 and 2012 IBC and IRC, as well as the flood requirements of ASCE 7-05, 7-10, and 24-05. The 8-page guide provides sections on preliminary considerations and design process, key flood terminology, and a 12-step process for incorporating flood resistance into the design of a building. This guide can be purchased from the International Code Council.

The source of the following information and requirements regarding the NFIP and the building codes cited above is *FEMA Quick Reference Guide; Comparison of Select NFIP and Building Code Requirements for Special Flood Hazard Areas* (2012b).

- The NFIP refers to the BFE for lowest floor elevation requirements, while the I-Codes and ASCE 24 refer to the Design Flood Elevation (DFE). The DFE is always the BFE or higher, depending on freeboard requirements.

- The NFIP, I-Codes, and ASCE 24 require the use of flood damage-resistant materials below the required lowest floor elevation

- The NFIP regulations do not have provisions for CAZs, but the I-Codes do. The IBC, by reference to ASCE 24, requires CAZ buildings to be treated like Zone V buildings. The IRC permits the use of ASCE 24 in the CAZ as an alternative to its flood provisions, which allows CAZ buildings to be treated like Zone V buildings. Starting in 2008, revised and new coastal FIRMs show the LiMWA, which delineates the landward limit of the CAZ.

- The NFIP requires that all buildings in Zone V resist the effects of wind and water loads acting simultaneously. The wind design requirements in the IRC are applicable in regions where the basic wind speed is under 110 mph or under 100 mph in hurricane-prone regions, which extend farther inland than Zone V in most areas.

- Both the NFIP and IRC require design certification in Zone V. Design certification is also required for breakaway walls that exceed a design safe loading resistance of 20 pounds per square foot.

- The NFIP and IBC/ASCE 24 allow *nonresidential* buildings in Zone A to be dry floodproofed. Residential buildings are not permitted to be dry floodproofed in any flood hazard zone. ASCE 24 includes limitations on the use of dry floodproofing and on measures that require human intervention.

There are no rules or requirements on how often a community must update its building code. The choice to update a code depends on the community's laws, needs, and politics. Communities do not generally update their building code every time an updated model code becomes available. In addition, some States do not legally have the ability to enforce a statewide mandatory adoption of a code.

The advantages for the community of updating its building code is that the design and construction requirements for flood-resistant structures (or flood- and wind-resistant structures in coastal areas) are built-in and explained in the code. If the community has a history of flood damage, it will be useful to provide copies of references 1 and 3 above to the local officials so that they can read about the more stringent requirements for flood resistance in a newer code.

Recommended meeting handouts include:

- Copies of the Building Science Toolkit CD

- Hard copies of the Toolkit spreadsheet tab for Building Codes

- Hard copies of the *Flood Resistant Provisions of the 2012 International Code Series* (FEMA 2012c)

- Hard copies of the *FEMA Quick Reference Guide; Comparison of Select NFIP and Building Code Requirements for Special Flood Hazard Areas* (2012b)

6.5 CONSULTATION COORDINATION OFFICER MEETING AND FLOOD MAP OPEN HOUSE

For Risk MAP projects that include regulatory map and FIS report updates, the CCO Meeting and Flood Map Open House are the last two official meetings. The CCO Meeting is hosted by the Project Team for the local officials receiving new or updated regulatory products, and the Open House is hosted by the Project Team and community officials to present the preliminary FIRM and FIS report to the public. The Project Team should hold these two meetings as soon as possible after the release of the new preliminary FIRM. A primary goal of Risk MAP is to promote community ownership of risk that will lead to promoting risk reduction and mitigation. To achieve this goal, the Project Team should use the CCO Meeting to provide community officials with resources and information to prepare them to more effectively share risk reduction messages and information with the public.

Table 6-6 provides information on the various elements of the CCO Meeting and Flood Map Open House.

Table 6-6: Elements of the CCO Meeting and Flood Map Open House

Element	Description
When held	Fourth of the four community Risk MAP meetings. Occurs during the preliminary NFIP Map Release and Mitigation Planning Phase.
Objectives	• Present preliminary FIRM to CCO Meeting and Open House attendees • Provide a brief explanation of the hydrologic analyses, hydraulic analyses, coastal analyses, alluvial fan analyses, or shallow flooding analyses that went into determining the flood hazards and depicting the results of the analyses on the FIRM • Review changes in flood hazard information from the effective FIS • Explain the FIS comment and appeals process • Discuss FIRM and FIS report maintenance after the effective date through LOMC • Present alternative outreach methods for the public to review the preliminary FIRM and FIS report and engage in the mitigation planning process (CCO Meeting only) • Discuss impact of insurance purchase, including grandfathering and the Preferred Risk Policy extension • Turn over the final Risk MAP products to the community
Recommended attendees for the CCO Meeting	• FEMA and the PTS • Select stakeholders, including community and tribal officials, before presenting the information to the public
Recommended attendees for the Flood Map Open House	• FEMA and the PTS • Individuals included in Discovery Meeting, Flood Risk Review Meeting (if held), and Resilience Meeting from the community receiving a new FIRM and FIS report • General public from the affected community (Open House only) • Other community officials interested in viewing the preliminary map from the affected communities • Media if appropriate
Activities	• Present an overview of revisions to FIRM panels and FIS report, including the CSLF product if not already presented • Discuss the appeals and comment process for regulatory products and the compliance/adoption timeline • Explain how revised FIRM panels may affect flood insurance premiums, including grandfathering options and Preferred Risk Policy extension • Explain how the new FIS information can be used as part of the mitigation planning process and coordinated with other planning activities related to future development, beneficial uses of the floodplain, and protecting sites of cultural, historic, and religious significance • Discuss outreach and risk communication tools available to the communities
Building Science objectives	Although the Building Science Objectives are better met at the Discovery and Resilience Meetings, the FEMA or study lead should be able to offer guidance and refer to the Building Science Toolkit if stakeholders want to discuss flood mitigation or get additional information.

CCO = Consultation Coordination Officer   FIS = Flood Insurance Study

CSLF = Changes Since Last FIRM   LOMC = Letter of Map Correction

FEMA = Federal Emergency Management Agency   NFIP = National Flood Insurance Program

FIRM = Flood Insurance Rate Map   Risk MAP = Risk Mapping, Assessment, and Planning

SECTION SEVEN   REFERENCES AND RESOURCES

7.1   REFERENCES

FEMA (Federal Emergency Management Agency). 2010. *Highlights of ASCE 24-05 Flood Resistant Design and Construction.*

FEMA. 2011a. Appendix I: *Discovery.* To be added to an updated version of FEMA, *Guidelines and Specifications for Flood Hazard Mapping Partners* (2003).

FEMA. 2011b. *Flood Resistant Provisions of the 2009 International Code Series.*

FEMA. 2011c. *Operating Guidance 3-11: Communicating Flood Risk with Risk MAP Datasets and Products.*

FEMA. 2011d. *Provisions of the 2009 I-Codes and ASCE 24 Compared to the NFIP.*

FEMA. 2012a. Appendix O, *Format and Standards for Non-Regulatory Flood Risk Products.* Draft. To be added to an updated version of FEMA, *Guidelines and Specifications for Flood Hazard Mapping Partners* (2003).

FEMA. 2012b. *FEMA Quick Reference Guide; Comparison of Select NFIP and Building Code Requirements for Special Flood Hazard Areas.*

FEMA. 2012c. *Flood Resistant Provisions of the 2012 International Code Series.*

S.K. Ghosh Associates, Inc. 2011. *CodeMaster for Flood Resistant Design.*

7.2   FEMA RESOURCES ON HAZARD-RESISTANT CONSTRUCTION

FEMA P-55, *Coastal Construction Manual, Volumes I and II* (2011)

FEMA P-259, *Engineering Principles and Practices for Retrofitting Flood-Prone Residential Structures (Third Edition)* (2012)

FEMA 347, *Above the Flood: Elevating Your Floodprone House* (2000)

FEMA P-348, *Protecting Building Utilities from Flood Damage: Principles and Practices for the Design and Construction of Flood Resistant Building Utility Systems* (1999)

FEMA P-424, *Design Guide for Improving School Safety in Earthquakes, Floods, and High Winds* (2010)

FEMA P-499, *Home Builder's Guide to Coastal Construction*, Fact Sheet 1.1, "Coastal Building Successes and Failures" (2010)

FEMA P-499, *Home Builder's Guide to Coastal Construction*, Fact Sheet 1.2, "Summary of Coastal Construction Requirements and Recommendations for Flood Effects" (2010)

FEMA P-499, *Home Builder's Guide to Coastal Construction*, Fact Sheet 1.5, "V Zone Design Certification" (2010)

FEMA P-499, *Home Builder's Guide to Coastal Construction*, Fact Sheet 2.1, "How Do Siting and Design Decisions Affect the Owner's Costs?" (2010)

FEMA P-499, *Home Builder's Guide to Coastal Construction*, Fact Sheet 2.2, "Selecting a Lot and Siting the Building" (2010)

FEMA P-499, *Home Builder's Guide to Coastal Construction*, Fact Sheet 3.1, "Foundations in Coastal Areas" (2010)

FEMA P-499, *Home Builder's Guide to Coastal Construction*, Fact Sheet 3.2, "Pile Design and Installation" (2010)

FEMA P-499, *Home Builder's Guide to Coastal Construction*, Fact Sheet 3.3, "Wood Pile-to-Beam Connections" (2010)

FEMA P-499, *Home Builder's Guide to Coastal Construction*, Fact Sheet 3.4, "Reinforced Masonry Pier Construction" (2010)

FEMA P-499, *Home Builder's Guide to Coastal Construction*, Fact Sheet 3.5, "Foundation Walls" (2010)

FEMA P-499, *Home Builder's Guide to Coastal Construction*, Fact Sheet 8.3, "Protecting Utilities" (2010)

FEMA P-499, *Home Builder's Guide to Coastal Construction*, Fact Sheet 9.1, "Repairs, Remodeling, Additions, and Retrofitting – Flood" (2010)

FEMA 543, *Design Guide for Improving Critical Facility Safety from Flooding and High Winds: Providing Protection to People and Buildings* (2007)

FEMA L-782, *Building Science for Disaster-Resistant Communities: Flood Hazard Publications* (2012)

FEMA P-787, *Catalog of FEMA Wind, Flood, and Wildfire Publications, Training Courses, and Workshops (Third Edition)* (2012)

FEMA Technical Bulletin 11, *Crawlspace Construction for Buildings Located in Special Flood Hazard Areas* (2001)

Recovery Advisory: Considerations for Rebuilding Your Flood-Damaged House (FEMA 2009)

Recovery Advisory: Initial Restoration for Flooded Buildings (FEMA 2005)

Recovery Advisory: The ABC's of Returning to Flooded Buildings (FEMA 2005)